MEASURE IT!

Measuring Distance

By T. H. Baer

Gareth Stevens
PUBLISHING

T0014480

Please visit our website, www.garethstevens.com. For a free color catalog of all our high-quality books, call toll free 1-800-542-2595 or fax 1-877-542-2596.

Library of Congress Cataloging-in-Publication Data

Baer, T. H., author.
 Measuring distance / T.H. Baer.
    pages cm — (Measure it!)
 Includes index.
 Audience: 6-7.
 Audience: K.
 ISBN 978-1-4824-3856-7 (pbk.)
 ISBN 978-1-4824-3857-4 (6 pack)
 ISBN 978-1-4824-3858-1 (library binding)
 1. Distances—Measurement—Juvenile literature. I. Title. II. Series: Measure it! (Gareth Stevens Publishing)
 TA601.B34 2016
 530.8—dc23

                                   2015026354

Published in 2016 by
Gareth Stevens Publishing
111 East 14th Street, Suite 349
New York, NY 10003

Copyright © 2016 Gareth Stevens Publishing

Designer: Laura Bowen
Editor: Ryan Nagelhout

Photo credits: Cover, p. 1 Ty Allison/Photographer's Choice/Getty Images; pp. 2–24 (background texture) style_TTT/Shutterstock.com; p. 5 Artush/Shutterstock.com; p. 7 (crayon) Mtsaride/Shutterstock.com; p. 9 (photo) Jasper Cole/Blend Images/Getty Images; p. 11 (left) Daniel Grill/Getty Images; p. 11 (right) Cyndi Monaghan/Moment/Getty Images; p. 11 (background rulers) SmileStudio/Shutterstock.com; pp. 15, 17, 19 (map components) Stockvector/Shutterstock.com; p. 21 (quarter) Abel Tumik/Shutterstock.com; p. 21 (dollar) nimon/Shutterstock.com.

Printed in the United States of America

CPSIA compliance information: Batch #CW16GS: For further information contact Gareth Stevens, New York, New York at 1-800-542-2595.

Contents

Boldface words appear in the glossary.

Between Points

Distance is the amount of space between two points. To figure out how much distance there is between things, you have to measure it. There are many different **units** we use to measure. Let's learn more about them!

An inch (in) is the smallest measurement in US customary, or standard, units. In the metric system, used in other countries, the millimeter (mm) is the smallest unit. A centimeter (cm) is 10 millimeters. Units can be **converted** from standard to metric.

measure

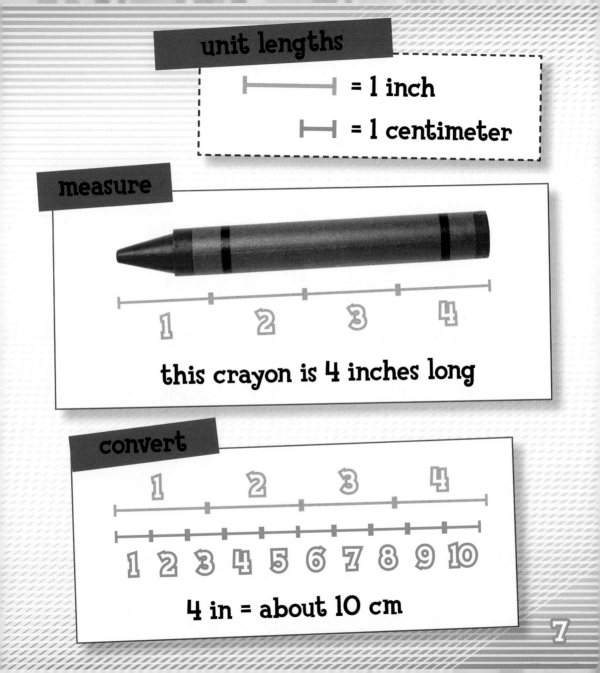

1   2   3   4

this crayon is 4 inches long

convert

1   2   3   4

1 2 3 4 5 6 7 8 9 10

4 in = about 10 cm

Getting Bigger

Twelve inches equal 1 foot (ft). Three feet make a distance called a yard (yd). A yard is also 36 inches. In the metric system, 100 centimeters equal a meter (m). A meter is also 1,000 millimeters.

US customary units	metric system units
inches	millimeters
feet	centimeters
yards	meters
miles	kilometers

Using a Ruler

You can use tools to measure short distances. One simple tool is a ruler. It usually measures 12 inches on one edge and about 30 centimeters on the other. Yardsticks are longer and measure 3 feet.

ruler

yardstick

11

Miles and Kilometers

A mile (mi) is the biggest unit we use to measure distance in the US customary system. A mile is 5,280 feet. Kilometers (km) are the biggest units of distance in the metric system. A kilometer is 1,000 meters.

conversion chart

US customary units		metric system units
1 inch	=	25.4 millimeters or 2.54 centimeters
1 foot or 12 inches	=	30.48 centimeters or 0.3048 meters
1 yard or 3 feet	=	0.9144 meters
1 mile or 5,280 feet	=	about 1,600 meters or 1.6 kilometers

Map Works

Maps have a **key** that shows a **scale** to help measure distance. For example, on this map 1 inch is equal to 2 miles. The house is 3 inches from the school on the map. This means the house is 6 miles from the school!

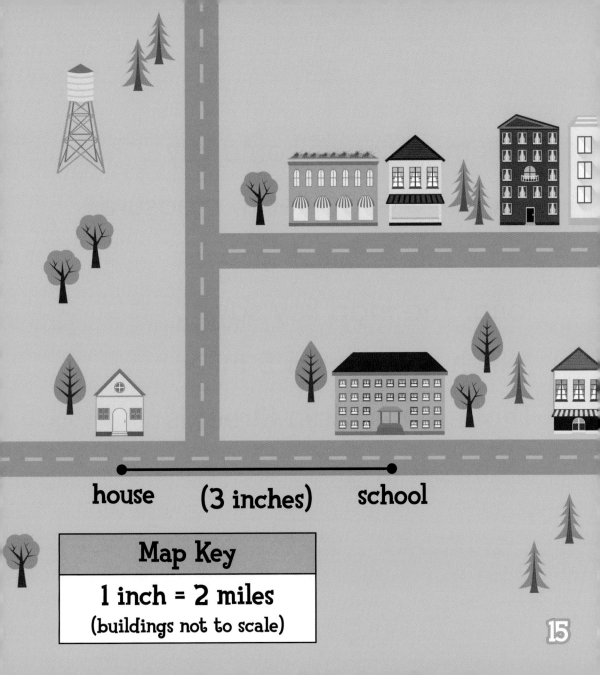

house (3 inches) school

Map Key

1 inch = 2 miles
(buildings not to scale)

15

This map shows some city streets. Use a ruler to measure Main Street. It's 3 inches long. The map key says 1 inch **represents** 5 miles. That means Main Street is 15 miles long!

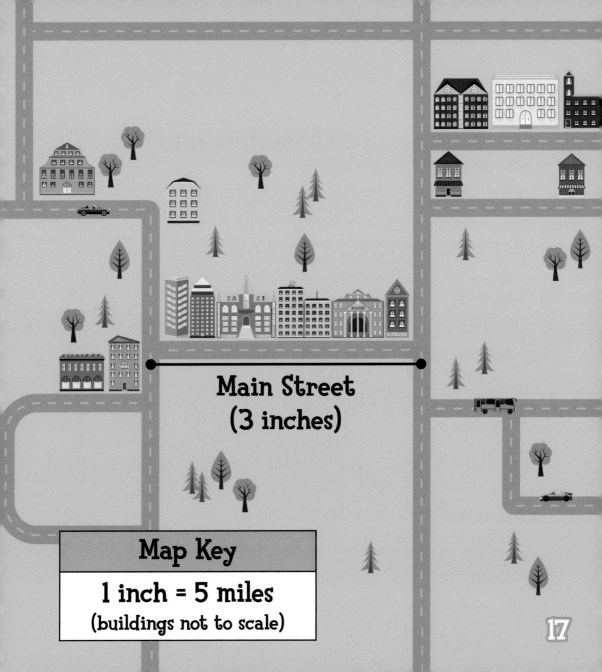

**Main Street
(3 inches)**

Map Key

1 inch = 5 miles
(buildings not to scale)

Some maps use kilometers and centimeters. Let's measure the distance between Town A and Town B. These towns are 3 centimeters **apart**. The map key says each centimeter represents 3 kilometers. The distance between the towns is 9 kilometers.

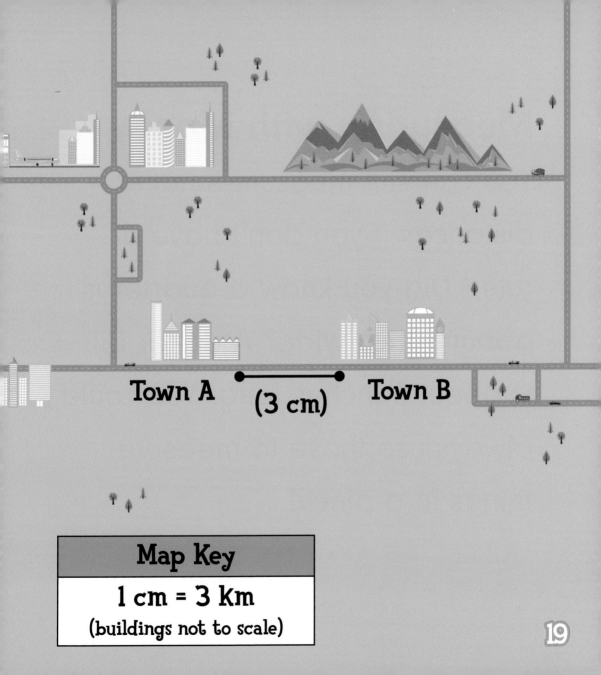

Town A

(3 cm)

Town B

Map Key

1 cm = 3 km

(buildings not to scale)

Measuring with Money

You can still measure smaller distances if you don't have a ruler! Did you know a quarter is about 1 inch wide? A dollar bill is about 6 inches long. You could always use those to measure things in a pinch!

about
1 inch

1

about 6 inches

Glossary

apart: away from one another

convert: to change from one unit to another

key: a list on a map that explains signs and pictures on the map

represent: to stand for

scale: a picture on a map that shows how much real distance the distance on the map equals

unit: a uniform amount for measuring

For More Information

Books

Adamson, Thomas K., and Heather Adamson. *How Do You Measure Length and Distance?* Mankato, MN: Capstone Press, 2011.

First, Rachel. *Measure It! Fun with Length & Distance.* Minneapolis, MN: ABDO Publishing, 2016.

Websites

Kids Math
ducksters.com/kidsmath/units_of_measurement_glossary.php
Find out more about different units of measurement on this site.

Measuring Distances
e-learningforkids.org/math/lesson/measuring-distances/
Learn how to use a ruler to measure maps on this interactive site.

Unit Lengths
numbernut.com/prealgebra/units-length.php
Find more conversions for different measurements here.

Index